Blockchain

The Future of All Database-Based Technology

Understanding The Technology Behind Bitcoin, Cryptocurrency, and Its Impact On Money, Business, & The World

The information herein is offered for informational purposes solely and is universal as so. The presentation of the information is without contract or any type of guarantee assurance.

The trademarks that are used are without any consent, and the publication of the trademark is without permission or backing by the trademark owner. All trademarks and brands within this book are for clarifying purposes only and are the owned by the owners themselves, not affiliated with this document.

Table of Contents

Introduction

Usually, when people think of money, they think of green pieces of paper that people use to buy and sell stuff. They think about online bank statements that are presented in numerical form.

More advanced thinkers would define financial statements and assets in terms of zeroes and ones located in some sort of remote hard drive or server. When people whip out their credit cards or make online payments, these digital records are changed.

Financial transactions have many different forms. They all go back to the basic and very old idea of a ledger. You don't have to be an accountant to have a basic understanding of ledgers.

Basically, it's a device where the amount of money you own is offset by the amount of money you spent and increased by the amount of money you put into your account. Ledger technology has been around for a very long time.

It works on a credit and debit system. In fact, a lot ancient cuneiform or clay tablet markings in Mesopotamia Involve financial transactions. For the longest time, people have been concerned with ledgers and their accuracy.

As you can imagine, if there is any kind of error in either writing to the ledger or checking the information in the ledger, there will be serious problems when people buy and sell stuff.

The historical problem with ledgers

As powerful as ledger technology is, there's always been one historical problem that it has suffered from for the longest time. It all boils down to recording. Usually, when there's a ledger, there's only one copy.

Maybe it's in a bank safety deposit box. Maybe it's in some sort of building. Maybe it's in some sort of government institution.

Please understand that ledgers can record all sorts of important transaction. We're not just talking about keeping track of credit and bank accounts. Ledgers area also used for insurance, real estate, and legal rights like contracts.

The problem is that regardless of how important the information they record and preserve, there's always the issue of fraud or unauthorized alteration. To a large degree, both parties in a ledger transaction have to trust each other.

One party would have a copy and the other party would have an individual copy. Those copies have to match. Often times, one party would lose their copy.

Maybe they would lose their passbook or maybe their computer would crash. Whatever the case may be, there has to be at least one copy that is easily accessible for this whole relationship to continue.

While the media that contains the ledger has evolved over time—from clay tablets, to stone, to papyrus paper, to vellum, to paper—the problem persisted. There are only two copies and both parties have to be rest assured that the part they're dealing with is honest enough.

The rise of Bitcoin

When Bitcoin became popular in recent years, a lot of the media attention to this technology focused on the idea of cryptocurrency. This is a currency or a store of value that was not backed by, or originated from some sort of governmental body. This was completely new.

For the longest time, money has to be backed by a government. In most cases, the value of any currency arises from the fact that a government can raise taxes with that currency and pay debts with that instrument.

Bitcoin was completely new because it had no physical backing. There was no paper, no metal coins, and no government backing it up.

The reason why the U.S. dollars are so powerful is because the U.S. government will honor the U.S. dollar. Its ability to print money as well as its ability to raise taxes gives the U.S. dollar its value.

People from all over the world who holds the green back can be rest assured that the U.S. government will take the U.S. dollar that they have as a form of payment. Of course, these foreign players don't usually the U.S. government any money.

They're not obligated to them, but the fact that the U.S. government stands by the greenback gives it value. This is called fiat currency.

In other words, it's just the word of the U.S. government giving value to that paper money. Prior to the rise of fiat currency, governments would actually redeem the pieces of paper that they issue as currency with hard assets like gold and silver.

Well, after the U.S. took the lead in getting off the gold standard, almost all of the world's currency is backed by specific governments, not any hard asset. Bitcoin was revolutionary because it's a store of value that people use to buy and sell stuff online that is not backed by any government.

Blockchain: the power of trust backing Bitcoin

This is where blockchain comes in. As I mentioned, if you understand my description of currencies above, it should become abundantly clear that for currencies to be worth anything, people have to trust the currency.

People have to feel that if the time comes for them to spend the currency, there will be somebody else paying value for that currency. In other words, there has to be a market for that currency.

This is the reason why people buy U.S. dollars and British pounds. They know that when they buy a U.S. dollar, it can be converted into a certain amount of their local currency. Depending on economic and political developments, they can actually get more local currency units for every single U.S. dollar they trade. This is how foreign exchange markets work.

You can either bet on the dollar by buying it and hoping that it will go up, or you can bet against the dollar by buying local currency and holding it, then trading it when the U.S. dollar crashes. Bitcoin is a complete break from this.

Again, it isn't backed by any hard asset or any government. Instead, it's backed by blockchain technology. That's all that it's backed by, but that did not prevent people from speculating on Bitcoin.

They actually trade real U.S. dollars and real world currencies for this type of cryptocurrency. So far, early adopters of Bitcoin have been handsomely rewarded.

It was only fairly recently that Bitcoin was worth a fraction of a cent. However, starting in 2017, the price of Bitcoin started to skyrocket until it hit a recent height near the $20,000 mark. It has crashed since then, but that's how wild speculation has become for Bitcoin.

For this multimillion dollar market to exist in the first place, one has to admit that Bitcoin has achieved a tremendous amount of legitimacy and this all goes back to blockchain.

<u>This book helps you understand the blockchain technology so you can get a clear idea on how it affects the valuation of money, the very definition of money, how trust is established and lost online, and its future impact on how we buy and sell stuff</u>.

Please understand that blockchain technology is so powerful and so profound that it's not just about cryptocurrency. In fact, it impacts any kind of database-based human record. This applies across the board.

We're not just talking about financial technology; we're also talking about insurance, legal records, and anything that requires a database, authentication, and verification. In other words, anything that has a shared database requires trust on both ends of the transaction.

Chapter 1: What is Blockchain Technology?

It's very easy to get confused between Bitcoin and the technology behind it, which is blockchain technology. To put it simply, blockchain is a technology that enables digital ledger of transactions that is very hard to corrupt.

It's programmed not just to record the financial transaction, but it offers easy-to-verify distributed architecture of all the transactions that took place within that ledger.

As I mentioned in the introduction, when you have a ledger, you basically have one copy in one location and another copy somewhere else. Often times, both parties suffer from recording issues and the ledgers do not match.

At that point, there has to be some sort of negotiation and the records have to be reconciled. Still, there has to be trust in the system for this to work.

With blockchain, you have a distributed database among a wide range of computes called nodes. When there is a transaction to be done in the ledger, this transaction is broadcast to all computers that have a software copy of the ledger.

This is a peer-to-peer computing network. Blockchain enables all the copies of the ledger located in a wide collection of computers distributed all over the world to validate the transaction.

These computers use an algorithm to validate the veracity of the transaction. This means that no one party can create a fake entry on the ledger unless all the computers agree on the truthfulness of the transaction.

This increases the trust both parties have on the transaction, as well as the record on the ledger. The verification doesn't just happen on one compute. It's a distributed through a peer-to-peer network all over the world.

This verification system was pioneered primarily for Bitcoin so that when people make purchases and it makes it all the way though the network, there is a tremendous amount of trust that that transaction actually happened and the balance that is publicly viewable is accurate.

Please note that this technology doesn't just apply for cryptocurrency. It can also be used for any kind of record that needs public accountability.

Once the transaction is verified, it is then added to a new block of data ledger. This is where blockchain gets its name. What you get is a publicly accessible, auto-encrypted chain of transactions using the same account.

This is processed and verified by many computers. All these computers can access the same list. When you conduct a transaction using Bitcoin, it's added to the latest entry or block in the ledger.

People can actually trace the account that you're using to see the account's past transactions. This technology's feature keeps everybody honest. When there is a common ledger that everybody can see and this ledger is vastly distributed among many different computers, it's harder to cheat the system.

What do the node owners get out of it?

Please understand that blockchain requires many different computers running the algorithm to verify transactions. This, of course, requires a lot of money, in terms of outlay. It also requires manpower in making sure that these computers are up and running around the clock on a 24/7 basis.

What do they get out of it? Well, here's the interesting thing about Bitcoin. I've described how blockchain technology works. However, Bitcoin is slightly different.

There has to be an incentive for the hardware operators to keep operating the computers that would verify all these Bitcoin transactions all over the world. When Bitcoin machine operators or owners run their system, there is a small chance that they will "mine" Bitcoin.

What happens is when they verify transactions; there is a race that's triggered to solve an algorithm problem. So, the more transactions you verify, the more algorithm puzzles, your network installation of the Bitcoin blockchain software, solves.

If your computer solves the puzzle, you get a Bitcoin. Considering the fact that Bitcoin is trading in the thousands of dollars, this provides a very real incentive for people to set up machines to run the open source Bitcoin blockchain software and process all these transactions.

Of course, this awarding of free Bitcoins happens randomly. However, it keeps enough incentive in the system for people to want to invest in the expensive hardware that keeps the distributed nodes alive.

What's so awesome about blockchain?

Now that you have a clear idea of how blockchain technology operates, what's the big deal? Well, first of all, it's not controlled by any single identity. This is a big deal.

When you have a bank account, you better hope that the bank has robust security technology. It should ensure that the ledger they use for your account remains intact.

This prevents scenarios such as a random person making changes, or a rogue employee taking money from your account and transferring it somewhere else. There's a tremendous amount of insecurity when financial transactions involve records that are under the control of one of the parties.

This arises from the fact that if the other party who's in control of the record screws up, there goes your financial security. If you have land titles, this is going to be a problem.

In fact, in the developing world, in countries like the Philippines, there are many cases of land titles going to court and causing litigation that takes decades because the registry of deeds went up in flames.

Usually, in some developing countries, when a registry of deed experiences a fire involving land titles, you can bet that land claims in court skyrocket. It's almost like clockwork. It's really a de facto land grab.

They know that since there are only two records of the land title, with one record being in the hands of the rightful owner, they can confidently come up with their own version of the land title once the centralized copy in the registry of deeds is burned. This causes a tremendous amount of headache.

It leads to all sorts of confusion and it costs a lot of money. It burns an unnecessary amount of money.

The great thing about blockchain is that there is no single point of failure. There really isn't. If the party that you're transacting with has a corrupt copy of your transaction, it won't bother you one bit because the record is distributed across thousands of computers all over the planet.

It's very hard to fake a land title using this technology. The same applies to a financial transaction because the fraudster or scammer can fake a few entries here and there, but he/she can't possibly fake all the entries distributed throughout nodes located all over the planet.

Unprecedented transparency

Let's get one thing clear. Bitcoin is very powerful, but also very weak at the same time. I know that sounds like an oxymoron, but it's absolutely true.

First, it's very powerful because, like I mentioned above, everything is transparent. When you create a new block of transaction using Bitcoin, everybody can see the trail of transactions that led to the current one.

It's as if everybody in the world can see what's going on with your wallet and this is what makes it weak. If the person looking works for the taxman, there's going to be issues. In fact, there are recent moves to track wallet activity with certain accounts.

For the longest time, Bitcoin was marketed as a 100% anonymous way of sending and receiving money through the internet. It's definitely a cheap way of sending money.

You can send hundreds of millions of dollars and spend only pennies in remittance costs. Usually, if you're sending thousands of dollars to places like India and the Philippines, you're going to have to pay a pretty hefty remittance fees.

The reason for this, of course, is that the transaction involves a traditional bank. Traditional banks charge a fee upfront when you send the money to a remittance center.

The transaction also goes through a foreign exchange conversion with the local bank, giving you a lower rate of exchange. To add insult to injury, by the time the money comes to the recipient, there is a processing fee on the other end.

All told, people pay through the nose for traditional remittance services. Bitcoin reduces all of the transaction friction to a few pennies.

That's why Bitcoin is a favorite of people who send hundreds of thousands of dollars regularly, but here's the problem. Often times, people who send that amount of money with such frequency are engaged in illegal activities.

It doesn't take rocket scientist to figure out those drug dealers, international prostitution traffickers, illegal pornographers, and other usual suspects love Bitcoin. It's a great way to launder illegal profits.

Not surprisingly, its public blockchain technology where you can track the transactions over time has become its Achilles' heel. Government tax authorities forced exchange companies to give up the wallet details or personally identifying details of their clients.

This means that the government tax authorities can now trace account holders' Bitcoin activities on a block by block basis. I hope you can see why this is a double-edged sword. On the one hand it provides a tremendous amount of transparency and accuracy. This keeps both parties of the transaction completely honest.

However, it also gives tax authorities a very powerful weapon to track down money laundering and other possibly illegal activities. There's really nothing the parties can do because it's all public recorded in the transaction blocks itself.

How do nodes operate?

Believe it or not, every computer that runs the open source blockchain software acts as some sort of administrator for the blockchain. Each node has to join up with other existing nodes, forming a network.

The big incentive, as I mentioned earlier, is that this nodes have a chance of mining Bitcoin or the blockchain software's currency. Technically speaking, they're not really mining Bitcoin. Instead, they're solving puzzles.

For each computational puzzle they successfully solve, a Bitcoin is produced by the winning computer. The upside to this lies in the market price of Bitcoin. This market price is set by Bitcoin exchanges.

These exchanges trade real U.S. dollars, euros, British pounds, and other real world currencies for Bitcoin. These currency exchanges have created a speculation market for Bitcoin.

Just how lucrative can Bitcoin mining be? Well, it all depends on the current price of Bitcoin. At its height, Bitcoin went north of $19,000. No joke.

When Bitcoin was first popularized, people can run the Bitcoin software on their computer and mine Bitcoins. In fact it was so easy to mine Bitcoins that the lowest price of Bitcoins was $0.08 in 2010. It briefly surged to $31 in 2011 to crash back down to $2.

It was doing this quite a bit. It would hit a high and then, it would crash back down. During this time, prior to 2017, it was fairly easy to mine Bitcoin because the nodes' network of computers running the open source Bitcoin technology software was fairly few.

As more and more people set up their computer to run this software, it got harder and harder to mine Bitcoin. Still, this created a massive distributed network that is hard to cheat.

It is so secure and resistant against manipulations precisely because of the size of the network. The more computers join the network, the more decentralized Bitcoin got and the harder it was to hack or tamper with.

No middleman

The most awesome thing about blockchain is the absence of middlemen in any kind of important financial transaction. It's easy to see the savings both parties stand to reap when they use blockchain technology to do financial transactions.

As I mentioned above, if you were sending, let's say a hundred thousand dollars to the Philippines, normally you would have to cough up a few hundred dollars, if not a couple of thousand dollars, in transaction fees.

This is due to the fact that you are going to have to route the money through brick and mortar enterprises and fixed bank accounts. These have high overheads. There's also the issue of foreign exchange conversion. It can get messy really quickly.

In Bitcoin, since there is no middleman between the person sending and the person receiving except the nodes, the fees are dramatically reversed. As I mentioned above, a recent transaction totaling millions of dollars costs a total of a few dollars in transaction fees using Bitcoin.

How's that for powerful and amazingly cheap transaction fees? You cut out the middle man. Well, the savings don't end there. If you use Bitcoin technology to transact land titles, you can come out lawyers. You probably don't need me to explain to you how much money you stand to save.

In the United States, real estate attorneys charge hundreds of dollars per hour. This translates to a tremendous amount of savings when land titles use a distributed blockchain technology, instead of lawyer's offices and land registration agencies.

You get all of the legal protections because you have a public record distributed over thousands of computers located all over the world. You're not relying on your lawyer to have a copy on a safety deposit box somewhere that mirrors the photo-film copy at your local deed registration office.

Make no mistake. Blockchain technology makes all sorts of financial transactions so much cheaper, so much faster, and so much more reliable.

Blockchain as a new Internet

If you think blockchain is already so amazing because of what it's one for financial and legal transactions, you haven't seen anything yet. The power of peer-to-peer computing networks has led to the use of the same architecture for transactions that are currently being done on the internet.

For example, eBay uses an auction system to put buyers and sellers together. If you have an old computer that you want to sell, you get on eBay and it essentially pools buyers and shows your ad.

If it's priced right or everybody bids correctly, you get a buyer. It's pretty straight-forward. It's called market-aggregation.

Here's the problem with market aggregation. You have one computer system in the middle. This is eBay's server. What happens if there is a virus in the system? What if there are hackers who captured important information or manipulated auctions?

Doubt enters the system and people are less likely to participate. People doubt that eBay is giving them the right price. They doubt that the authenticity of the products.

Do you see the problem of a one too many model? That is the model of a lot of exchanges and platforms on the internet. You basically have one computer and many other users, whether they're buyers or sellers, plugging in to that computer network.

Blockchain stands to reengineer how these services are structured. Imagine if eBay or the software running eBay did not just exist on a network of computers that are controlled by one company. What if this auction system was distributed over hundreds of thousands of computer?

Given how block chain makes each transaction transparent and immune to hacking, this distributed architecture might actually make the eBay business model more bullet-proof. It also makes it more accessible to people all over the world.

Most importantly, it can reduce transaction costs. This also applies to PayPal. Currently, if you receive payments via PayPal, you pay through the nose. Not only is your payment reduced by the foreign exchange rate PayPal uses, but you also have to pay a fee for using PayPal.

What if this system uses a blockchain technology? eBay has the same fee structure. By using eBay, you have to pay a transaction fee and there are additional fees that you have to pay.

Another application of a blockchain distributed technology involves crowd funding. **GoFundMe** and **Kickstarter** are very popular crowd funding platforms.

If somebody gets in an accident or goes to jail and needs a legal fund going, their friends and family members can go to GoFundMe and hold a fundraising event. Maybe the money is going to be spent on an operation or a defense lawyer.

Whatever the case may be, they go on a platform and this platform sends the word out to a wide number of people and these people plug in to the same platform. Again, the same eBay one too many structure is apparent.

What if there is a distributed platform where people can donate funds using this distributed platform. They can donate by using cryptocurrency or traditional currency.

File storage using blockchain

Another powerful application of blockchain technology involves file storage. The problem with traditional internet file storage should be obvious.

If you store a file on your Google Drive, you better hope and pray that Google's distributed server network properly backs up and preserves your data.

Now, Google has a massive network located all over the world. It also has a tremendous amount of money to make sure that the network is virus-free, secure form hackers, and doesn't experience blackouts.

That's all well and good. However, the problem is that since there's only one company in charge of that network. We're back to the same One-To-Many architecture. Sure, the one network in the middle is very robust, but it still essentially involves many participants dealing with one central structure.

Blockchain can democratize file storage. Of course, there are security issues here because you would not want sensitive files appearing transparently on the blockchain public ledger. You wouldn't want the government seeing what's inside your files.

Still, distributed blockchain-based global file storage system offers a lot of promise. In fact, there is already a system that is being pioneered called the interplanetary file system.

This is very similar to how torrents work. Torrents were pioneered to use private computers to create networks to share files. This was a very powerful and fast way to move large blocks of data.

Unfortunately, it was primarily used for piracy. People were sharing movies and music using torrents. Can you imagine using blockchain for file storage with the same incentive system?

This means that instead of your payoff coming in the form of a full copy of Breaking Bad or The Sopranos, you actually make money running the file system blockchain software on your spare computer.

This is still in its infancy because the incentives may not be strong enough for people to want to devote such hardware firepower to such a system. Maybe a better approach would be to charge money for the data storage.

Then, allocate the pay-outs of that distributed tool of subscriber fees to individual node operates based either on a random distribution system, through computation puzzles, or some other scheme. If the incentives of this distributed file storage network get ironed out, this can prove to be a very powerful alternative to Google Drive or other centralized file storage systems.

Chapter 2: How Bitcoin Works

Please understand that blockchain is the technology powering bitcoin. Bitcoin is a cryptocurrency that uses blockchain technology. It is not blockchain itself. These two have been closely interlinked, and in the minds of too many people, they're one and the same. No, they're not.

Blockchain is a technology. It is a way of managing an online ledger. That's all it is.

You can put all sorts of stuff on the ledger, and you can operate the ledger in many ways. The ledger can also govern many different types of behavior and produce different types of outcomes.

Blockchain is a technology. Bitcoin is a specific implementation of blockchain technology.

This chapter talks about the most famous example of blockchain technology. Prior to bitcoin, blockchain basically existed only in theory.

There are at least a couple of white papers out there that describe, in general terms, how this peer to peer ledger management technology called blockchain is supposed to work.

But when bitcoin came on to the scene, the world all over had a working model of how blockchain can actually work and its massive potential, not just for moving money or value around, but also for non-financial transactions.

This chapter describes how bitcoin works.

Step #1: Install a bitcoin wallet on your computer or mobile device

Bitcoin software works on desktop, laptop or mobile devices like tablets and mobile phones. When you do this, you will get a bitcoin address.

This is your digital wallet. This number is your identity on the bitcoin network.

Once people have your bitcoin number, they can send payment to you. If your friends need money from you, they send you their number.

It's not much different from how email functions. But unlike email, bitcoin addresses are only used once.

Step #2: Send money through the blockchain

A blockchain is a distributed digital ledger that all computers running the bitcoin software synchronize.

Bitcoin has an open source software that would-be bitcoin miners and node operators would install on their computer networks.

Once this open source software is installed on a computer, it starts talking to other computers that have the same bitcoin open source software installed. It then starts to synchronize itself to the other computers running bitcoin software in the network.

All the transactions involving bitcoin are stored in this shared public ledger called the blockchain. It enables people with a bitcoin wallet to determine how much balance is left on their account. This then enables them to spend that amount.

All the transactions that run through the network are verified through the blockchain. The ledger is set up to prevent anybody from deducting twice from the same account at the same time. In other words, it prevents fraud or unauthorized transactions.

The blockchain uses algorithm puzzles to verify transactions

When a person with a bitcoin wallet wants to send money to another party, the transaction takes place on an exchange, and the bitcoin wallet of the person sending bitcoin "signs" the transaction using their wallet's secret data called a digital seed or private key.

This signing process triggers a mathematical calculation, which proves to the network that the transaction took place between two people who actually own the two wallets engaged in the transaction.

This mathematical proof creates a signature that locks the transaction so that once the transaction record is entered into the blockchain; it cannot be changed by any third party.

People with two bitcoin wallets who engage in a transaction through an exchange; end up broadcasting their transaction to the complete network. This whole process usually is verified and recorded in the blockchain within a 10-20 minute time span.

Bitcoin's developers call this transaction process "mining" because the computers who run bitcoin's software to verify and record this transaction can solve computer puzzles, which randomly award bitcoins.

So, by performing this verification service for the entire network, each and every computer on the system is rewarded with a random chance to actually get a bitcoin for its processing work. This process is dubbed "mining."

How Mining Works

Mining doesn't occur on a one to one basis. The whole network of computers that have bitcoin open source software installed are all performing these mathematical computations to solve mathematical problems associated with confirmation and verification of transactions pending within the network.

This includes matching up the keys in the transaction to verify that these actually came from verified accounts and that the claimed owners are who they truly are based on their keys. And once these transactions are confirmed, the record of these transactions are then recorded in the blockchain.

The blockchain is a chronological set of transactions that can be verified by the computers running bitcoin software. This neat, orderly and chronological sequence of the blockchain enables all the computers in the network to verify and agree to the state of the complete network.

This means they have a frame of reference as to which transactions happen and what sequence they are always synchronizing to that sequence.

A transaction is only valid once the blockchain confirms the transaction. This happens when the details are packed in a data block which has to meet certain computational rules.

These are based on cryptographic that node computers have to solve for them to pack the block in the series of blocks that make up the blockchain.

This is a very tricky way of making sure that previous blocks in the chain are not altered because they passed a cryptographic test. These are very strict rules that dictate whether a block fits or not.

So, if a block is modified earlier in the chain, it would invalidate all blocks that are produced after that point because they don't pass the cryptographic test. This is the mining process that is synchronized across the network.

So, all the other computers see that these blocks are being produced and they must pass the cryptographic rules distributed throughout the network.

All computers run the same cryptographic rule. If a hacker contaminated, let's say, 10% of the bitcoin network, the hack will still fail.

Because the hacker will try to modify the blocks, maybe erase transactions, change transaction details, but they can easily be detected because 90% of the network is still synchronized and using the official copy of the blockchain that passed the cryptographic rules and verification system. This prevents any alternation to the system.

The verification performed by the network ensures that the blocks are all verified and legit. This is called the mining process because all these computers are being managed for selfish purposes.

The people running these computers and running up all these electricity bills as well as paying for labor are not doing this for their health. Instead, when they run these computers, it is with the understanding that they're engaged in some sort of competitive lottery.

There is a chance that when they let the computer mine by verifying transactions and thereby protecting the integrity of the blockchain, they will be rewarded with a bitcoin. Considering how much bitcoin has gone up in value, this can be quite a profitable activity for network operators.

Since all the computers in the network are essentially competing with each other to come up with the proof of work that verifies transactions, this prevents any group of people or any individual from controlling what is included in the blockchain. Because they operate for their own self-interest, distribute throughout the world, and run these computerized puzzles to verify the blockchain.

Even if somebody were to come in and try to control as many different computers as possible, they can't because the network is so huge and so decentralized.

Also, any kind of alteration will be quickly found out because the whole network verifies all transactions as they compete for a random award of a bitcoin.

The Weaknesses of Bitcoin's Implementation of Blockchain Technology

It's easy to get excited about bitcoin because we're talking about something that went from a value of less than 25 US cents to close to $20,000. What's not to get excited about?

But please understand that bitcoin is actually operating on a 10-year old blockchain technology.

Ever since the implementation of bitcoin, blockchain technology has continued to evolve. There are other implementations, in particular, Ripple and IBM blockchain that are so much faster than bitcoin.

In fact, bitcoin's technology is so old that it actually needs around 10 minutes to produce a single data block in the blockchain. This boils down to about 7 transactions per second. That may seem like a lot, but it's very slow compared to other blockchain technology platforms.

For example, Google's Ripple cryptocurrency has blockchain technology that processes 1,500 transactions per second. IBM's own blockchain technology cranks out 1,000 transactions per second.

Processing speed is the most obvious weakness of bitcoin. This is why it's unfair for critics of bitcoin to automatically assume that blockchain is slow.

Please understand that bitcoin is not blockchain. Blockchain is an independent technology. Bitcoin is just one implementation of that technology. In fact, bitcoin is a 10-year old implementation technology.

The state of the art in blockchain technology is quite impressive because it's able to process transactions so much faster.

Huge Energy Requirements

Another worrying weakness of bitcoin's blockchain implementation is its heavy energy use. Given bitcoin's processing inefficiencies, it requires a huge network of computers and this, of course, translates to a tremendous amount of electricity being used up.

It is not a surprise that a lot of environmental activists are saying that bitcoin technology is not environmental friendly. Because if you have all this massive network of computers sucking up a tremendous amount of electricity, and this electricity is generated by coal or fossil fuels or other dirty non-renewable sources of electrical energy, then it can have a tremendously negative impact on the environment.

It has been claimed that bitcoin has a very worrisome carbon footprint. This is true of bitcoin. Make no mistake, bitcoin's blockchain implementation is guilty as far as its negative impact on the environment is concerned.

This is due to the fact that bitcoin's mining process needs a proof of work to validate transactions.

Basically, the keys involved between two wallets go through cryptographic rules, which is essentially a puzzle that the computer has to solve, and this burns up a tremendous amount of processing power. This mathematical algorithm is needed by the bitcoin network to maintain the integrity of its blockchain.

Unfortunately, this burns up a tremendous amount of energy because of the computation power required. In fact, according to some estimates, the total bitcoin global network burns up the same amount of energy that the country of Denmark uses in a year.

Newer cryptocurrencies deal with the proof of work portion of transaction verification differently. Ethereum uses proof of stake instead of proof of work.

Proof of stake essentially looks at validating transactions by using the age of the coins in the network as well as the size of the stake involved in the chain. Bitcoin, on the other hand, requires nodes to solve puzzles in exchange for a newly mined coin.

This basically works up the whole network, while proof of stake simply consults the whole network and comes up with a computation based on the state of the network. This leads to less energy because it spares the whole network from having to solve a computation puzzle.

Structural Incentive Problems

In addition to burning up a tremendous amount of energy as well as its slow speed, bitcoin suffers from really serious incentive-based structural problems.

The total number of bitcoins that can be actually mined is set to a hard limit of 21 million bitcoins. According to some estimates, the network will have mined this by the year 2140.

The problem with this is that even before 2140 arrives, there will be a point in time where member computers of the globally distributed bitcoin network will no longer find it worthwhile to continue mining because the chances of mining a new bitcoin has become so astronomically distant that, from a purely return on investment perspective, it just doesn't make any sense to continue mining, which means it doesn't make any sense for them to continue to be part of the bitcoin network.

If you add to this the fact that bitcoin's technology requires proof of work, which burns up a tremendous amount of computational energy, it's easy to see that the bitcoin network can quickly become unprofitable for individual nodes.

Whatever transaction fees are created by the total network will not be enough to cover the upkeep costs of member nodes in the network, much less generate them a profit.

Eventually, based solely on business reasons, a large chunk of the bitcoin network will cease operations. This means that mining will become slower and slower as more and more bitcoin network nodes disconnect from the network.

This is a serious problem because transactions would then take longer and longer to process. Since the value of bitcoin is locked into the power of the network to process transactions, there is an open question as to whether the value delivered by this network, as slow as it will be as it's closer to 2140, would be worth the bother.

This is a serious problem because you have to remember that currencies gain their value based on consumer perception. If people all over the world think that the US dollar is worth something, then the US dollar is worth something.

But once they lose confidence on a currency, its value drops like a rock. You only need to look at the currency crisis faced by countries like Argentina and Zimbabwe to understand how this works.

Now, if the value of bitcoin revolves completely around the ability of its network to process transactions, what will happen to that perceived value when the network becomes so slow that transactions take forever to process?

This really boils down to service valuation. If I'm buying a service from you and it takes you forever to deliver that service, and when compared to other competing services out there your work quality isn't all that good, how much value would I put in your operations?

Bitcoin's Use as a Store of Value is Dependent on Transaction Volume

Paradoxically enough, when bitcoin was very cheap, its transaction volume was very high and the system performed very quickly. When bitcoin exploded in value, later half of 2017, bitcoin transactions actually fell through the floor. This signals a key structural weakness in the use of bitcoin as a form of stored value.

To put it simple, if you plan to use bitcoin as a form of currency, this is going to be a problem because you want a stable value for whatever currency you're using. And since transaction volumes have crashed through the roof as the price of bitcoin has gone up, this has actually made bitcoin very vulnerable to exchange price fluctuations.

It's going to be very hard to use bitcoin as a currency when its price goes haywire. It's really bipolar in terms of volatility.

The Verdict is Still Out on Bitcoin

Just like with any innovative product, there is no shortage of bitcoin true believers out there. These are people who truly believe that bitcoin is the epitome or the state of the art of blockchain-based cryptocurrency technology.

Well, as you can tell by the analysis above, that is hardly the case. Bitcoin has been around for a decade, and blockchain technology has not exactly stood still. It has evolved in terms of verification power, verification methods, and most importantly, network resource demand.

Bitcoin technology burns up a lot of processing power because of its proof of work requirement. This slows down transactions and it also puts a damper on the number of transactions bitcoin can do per second.

It also sets in motion practical considerations that may lead to the death of a significant chunk of the bitcoin network. This can then lead to doubts regarding the usage of bitcoin as a store of value or as a means of verifying transactions in the first place.

In other words, it would not be outside of the realm of possibility for bitcoin to be viewed as worthless because of the design limitations of the software that it's running.

The distributed developers working together on bitcoin's open source software do have a technology called **"lightning"** that they're working on that's supposed to take care of these bottlenecks.

The jury is still out on the ultimate fate of bitcoin. Until and unless it's able to solve these problems, then it may become the victim of its own success. Still, this does not in any way mean that bitcoin will crash down to zero value tomorrow or any time soon.

As I have mentioned above, there are still a tremendous amount of bitcoin true believers out there who sincerely believe that, since bitcoin is a first mover in the blockchain technology, that fact alone insulates it, to a large degree, from more efficient and faster competitors who came later like Ethereum.

I wish I could tell you that it's very easy to see from current patterns what the road ahead looks like. But it isn't.

Considering how fast blockchain technology is evolving, given the fact that big companies like Google and IBM are constantly improving on their own version of blockchain, there is only one thing that most people can agree on: blockchain will continue to be exciting in the foreseeable future because the number of applications, blockchain technology can be used for, continues to grow by the day.

Bitcoin, on the other hand, is a different matter entirely. It has its own implementation, which in turn brings its own set of problems. It also has its own benefits.

So, it's a good idea at this point to just look at bitcoin and blockchain's evolution as running on two completely different tracks. The fate of one does not necessarily have to dictate what happens to the other.

Chapter 3: Long Term Structural Challenges for Blockchain Technology

In the previous chapter, we talked about bitcoin and the challenges it faces. As you can tell, these challenges are definitely not easy. They're not going to go away anytime soon.

Until and unless there is a tremendous shift in bitcoin's underlying block chain technology, it's anybody's guess how long bitcoin will be viewed as a worthwhile store of value. That's just a fancy way of saying it's only a matter of time until people will decide whether bitcoin is worth anything.

As alarming as that may seem, please understand that blockchain technology in of itself is not free of challenges either. As exciting as this shared digital ledger knowledge may be at many levels, it faces some serious structural challenges.

Here are just some of them. I'm not going to pretend that this is a comprehensive list of all the possible problems blockchain technology will face in the future or is currently facing. However, these are the most significant and most important.

The problem of incentive

Please understand that the reason blockchain is so amazing is because there are so many machines running the same software that validates and verifies transactions in the network. It's very hard to trick the system because it's so big, so vast and so widespread that even if you were to successfully pack a fraction of the network, you still have to deal with the verification done by the rest of the network.

The reason for this is that this installed network of software is routinely doing calculations for every transaction going through the system. It keeps the system honest.

As I mentioned in the discussion about bitcoin, energy usage is an issue here, but the good news is thanks to the rise of alternative cryptocurrency technology like Ethereum, there are more efficient ways to get the kind of result that bitcoin's "proof of work" process achieves.

Even then, there's still a bigger problem. There is an eight-hundred-pound gorilla in the room that we need to address for blockchain technology to truly progress and spread beyond cryptocurrency uses.

The big issue here is incentive. Since this network requires a tremendous amount of people to install this open-source software on their computers, it has to have a compelling way to incentivize these people. Put simply, any kind of blockchain software must answer these individuals' burning question, "What's in it for me?"

It's easy to understand how third-party users can benefit from a distributed blockchain-based network. You can save money on transaction costs, you can verify transactions very quickly and you can store files without losing any sleep because you know you can retrieve it once it's fully synced across the network.

Most people understand out but the problem is what is the incentive or the advantage for the people running this network. With cryptocurrency, they get coins.

Bitcoin is so big and so popular because there are so many people running the bitcoin software in the hopes that they would successfully "mine" a bitcoin. At six thousand bucks a pop, that is quite an incentive.

Well, what if you are just starting a blockchain-based network and you're not using it for cryptocurrency purposes? This is a very high likelihood because as of this writing, there are thousands of wannabe bitcoins out there.

That hat implementation is pretty much beat to the ground. The last thing this world needs is yet another wannabe cryptocurrency coin.

Unless you come up with something completely different as far as how you implement and manage the underlying blockchain technology behind your coin, you're late to the party.

This means that non-cryptocurrency users must provide enough rewards to people installing their blockchain-based software; otherwise, the network is not going to get built.

Remember people are always asking, "What's in it for me? Is the amount of money that I will make installing your blockchain-based software on my computer to become part of your network going to be enough to offset my costs?"

The costs are quite significant. We're not just talking about the hardware involved, which, of course involves the computer, but we also are talking about recurring costs like electricity, manpower, security precautions, possibly insurance. Do you see how this works?

The costs are significant. That's why any new implementation of blockchain technology must provide enough incentive to the nodes that make up the network.

What makes this really problematic and challenging is the fact that the bigger the network, the smoother the operation of the system will be. This increases the likelihood that more people will use the system.

Maybe it's for storing files. Perhaps it's for providing some type of service. Possibly, it involves facilitating some sort of online sale. Whatever the implementation may be there has to be enough people in the network; otherwise it's going to be too slow and too insecure.

Please understand that whenever you put everything on some sort of public ledger, there's always the risk that the network can get compromised because hackers may access enough of the nodes to cause some serious damage.

You end up stuck at some level or other with the classic chicken-and-egg problem. Potential node participants are not going to go through the time, hassle and expense of installing your blockchain technology-based software on their network or single computer if they can't get any assurance that they will get something out of it.

This causes a problem because third-party consumers won't be excited to use your system because the network is too small. Something's got to give. There has to be enough built-in incentives for people to want to take a risk with your technology.

Transparency in data ownership

Another problem with blockchain technology is the fact that it has to be transparent enough to all nodes running the software so transactions going through the network would be verified rapidly.

This means the more transparent the transactions, which means less encryption, the faster the network can run provided enough machines are running the software.

At the other end of the equation is security. You don't want people to get enough details of the transaction in your network that it may lead to hacking or some serious compromise later on if, for some reason, the hackers take control of enough machines in the network. While this is a remote possibility because of the encryption involved in most blockchain software, this is still a threat that has to be dealt with. How do you balance the need for systemic efficiency, which requires less encryption in a more transparent system and full security?

This is a serious problem because people are less likely to participate in your network if they feel that the information that's being shared is too easy to figure out or intercept.

This is not an easy problem to solve because if you were to use blockchain technology on a purely enclosed basis, meaning you own all the machines running the software, then you probably would be better off using other distributed processing software out there. There's really no need to use blockchain.

The whole point behind blockchain is you're going to be building a network running on other people's computers. Everybody's connecting through this network and pooling their computing resources. That's not the case if you are just going to end up controlling or owning all the computers running your blockchain software.

How do you get people to sign on given the difficulty of presented by either extremely slowly processing because the system is heavily encrypted and very secure on the one hand and possible security breaches because you're prioritizing speed over security? This is not an easy problem to solve.

Moreover, if you were to pack in a tremendous amount of security into your blockchain, this can burn up a tremendous amount of resources as far as computing power goes. This, in turn, triggers the incentive issue that I discussed above.

You better give people a very good reason they should install your software. It has to lead to some sort of benefit to them. This is a very hard case to make for people who are going to be using your system for a one-off or rare transaction.

For example, if I just need something done once, let's says, for a year, it probably is not worth my time to install software that will run for the whole year just so I can do that one thing.

The reward that you offer must be consistent and must be constant.

The threat of regulation

As evidenced by the recent European Union regulations regarding data privacy, people from all over the world are getting increasingly worried about data privacy. This started in Europe but don't think for a second that it's going to stay there.

As more and more jurisdictions develop fears regarding the improper use of consumer mass-scale data, there will be more and more restrictions on how this data is collected, processed, used and transferred.

If you're thinking of building a new technology based on a blockchain data management structure, you might want to think twice because the network that you build might end up getting so heavily regulated that it might not be worth your time.

It would be great if the big legal challenge to blockchain strictly took the form of fines registration fees but, oftentimes, regulators require something more expensive. I am, of course, talking about your time.

If it turns out that you have to jump through so many regulatory hoops, and you have to make so many filings and come up with so many records and paperwork, it might not be worth anybody's time to build a blockchain-based technology using a distributed data network. The paperwork costs and matching potential fines and criminal liability may not make it worthwhile.

In theory, it may seem like you'll be able to handle all sorts of things to make people's lives so much smoother and more sufficient, but given the bureaucratic and regulatory costs involved in policing that data, making sure that you collect only a bare minimum data or you use data only in a certain way can prove to be a bit too much.

Long-term investor interest is not guaranteed

I'm not going to lie to you. The reason this book even exists is because blockchain technology right now is red hot. It seems like technology journalists and media players cannot talk enough about blockchain.

This is one topic that is on top of everybody's mind. A lot of people are convinced that this is the next big thing. A lot of people have called it the killer app.

Well, it's easy to see why a lot of the startup companies being facilitated through AngelList and other platforms involve blockchain technology. It seems that the more people talk about blockchain, the more investors are willing to step up and put down solid money for further implementation of this technology.

As it stands, it appears there's more investor money available than viable ideas that can be funded. If you are all familiar with how venture firms pick startup companies to invest in, it really all boils down to two things: how hot the underlying idea is and the competence and proven track record of the founders looking to capitalize on that idea.

Make no mistake there are many startup companies out there that have seemingly groundbreaking, earth-shattering and truly revolutionary ideas. Unfortunately for them, a lot of venture funds and professional investors would not touch them with a ten-foot pole.

Their founders are simply unknown quantities. The venture community doesn't quite know what to make of these companies because the founders are simply too new or unknown.

Of course, there are simple solutions around this. The founders can patch together enough cash to hire a CEO with some industry name recognition. They can get the backing of an angel investor who has connections within the venture community.

There are many ways to get around this problem, but still, the entrepreneurial pedigree of the founders of blockchain-based technologies is often put under a microscope.

These go hand in hand. You have to have both a good idea that is explained very clearly, and you must convince potential investors that you know what you're doing or, at the very least, that you're competent enough to turn the idea from a mere concept to a product or service that people would actually pay good money for.

Right now, blockchain is red hot. It seems that venture funds as well as individual investors are running around in circles looking for the latest and greatest blockchain startup to invest some money in.

The problem is as more blockchain-based startups make the rounds, a lot of this venture appetite would have been satisfied. Also, as the technology matures to the point that companies that hype it up or brag about its usage begin to hit walls, experience growth pains or flat-out fail, it's anybody's guess how long the investor community will remain excited about this technology.

This has happened before. I remember when the Apple iPhone originally launched. There were tons of app companies being formed in the years following 2007. It's as if there was a massive rain, and after a day or two, all these mushrooms popped up all over the place.

That's the impression you got because all these technologies were saying the right words like app distributed processing and gamification. They were saying the right concepts to target the investor demand and, sure enough, after a few years, most of these companies went belly up.

What do you think the investors felt? A lot of them felt burnt. A lot of them became gun-shy. Now, this doesn't mean that they didn't want to invest in technology anymore, but as the old saying goes, fool me once, shame on you; fool me twice, shame on me.

Please understand that the investor excitement behind blockchain is actually third-wave excitement as far as venture capitalists and angel investors are concerned.

The first wave, of course, was around the year 2000 when Internet companies were all the rage, and people were just throwing money at any company that has something to do with the Internet.

It doesn't matter how remote the connection is. People were just willing to invest in companies that claimed to be connected with Internet technology. At that point, investors really did not know what they were and, sure enough, the market peaked and it crashed. A lot of people lost a tremendous amount of money.

The second wave happened right after the Apple iPhone made mobile phone technology a commonplace. This exploded the market, and a lot of app developers popped up. People got burned there as well. For every WhatsApp, which sold for billions of dollars to Facebook, there were literally hundreds of thousands of other failed companies that produced apps.

Now, we have bitcoin and blockchain technology. The same process is happening, but investors are gun-shy.

Now, don't get me wrong. I'm not saying that they won't invest or they're less likely to invest. Instead, they're more likely to ask a lot of questions.

If you are reading this book because you want to build new solutions that tap into the tremendous distributed processing potential of blockchain technology, you need to be aware of this fact. You need to be aware that you're going to be hit with a wide range of questions. You better be prepared for them.

While it's easy to anticipate basic questions like "How are you going to make money? When do you expect your company to be profitable? What are you going to use the investment fund for?" There are other questions that you may not be able to answer.

Be on the lookout for questions about the scalability of your system, dealing with security issues and, most importantly, dealing with the fundamental structural problems I've raised above.

You have to understand that when venture funds invest in one blockchain technology company, after another, they become better experts. They are able to identify weak spots that tend to persist from company to company despite seeming differences in their business models.

You have to anticipate this. You have to be ready for this. Otherwise, you probably are not going to get funded.

Believe me there's nothing more discouraging than going through several investor presentations and seed funding roadshows only to come up empty-handed.

On top of all of this, please understand that you're not exactly alone in thinking up of blockchain-based ideas. Ideas are a dime a dozen. Anybody can come up with an idea.

In fact, two people might come up with similar-sounding ideas, but please understand that you're not going to be getting funding based on how sweet or smart-sounding your idea is.

Instead, the likelihood of you getting any significant funding turns on implementation.

This is a serious problem because, again, it opens a chicken-or-egg issue. If you don't get funding, you can't get proof of concept. This is especially true if you have something very big and complicated in mind. Without a proof of concept, you can't get funding. Do you see how this works? This is the kind of catch-22 that kills a lot of blockchain-based tech dreams.

I'm sharing this with you so you can be prepared. I'm not at all trying to discourage you or depress you. However, you have to understand that this is always in the mix. You have to anticipate this.

You have to have your answers ready because, at the end of the day, there are many founders and entrepreneurs competing for a limited pile of investor money. You have to overcome the competition. You have to come up with better answers.

This doesn't mean that your idea has to be the best. Oftentimes, it all boils down to being the first to market with a truly commercial working system and the first to monetize.

Make no mistake the whole idea of an online store is not unique to Amazon.com. Neither is the idea of paying third-parties to promote the products on your store through affiliate links.

However, Amazon was able to take these two ideas and run with them to gain very important advantages that basically left its competitors in the dust. Now, Amazon is a company worth hundreds of billions of dollars.

It's not the idea. It's the implementation. That should give you quite a bit of hope. So, focus more on how practical your idea is, how cheap it is to implement and how scalable it is instead of how unique it is.

Believe me if you were to sit down and put in the time, I'm sure you can come up with a unique mouse trap. However, people are not necessarily looking for a new mouse trap. They're just looking for something that works and doesn't cost a lot of money. I hope you get my point.

Chapter 4: Blockchain as a Financial Technology Backbone Infrastructure

The title of this chapter pretty much says it all. It doesn't mention Bitcoin. It doesn't dwell on cryptocurrencies.

As you already know, when people talk about blockchain, it's usually in the context of cryptocurrencies like Bitcoin. After all, Bitcoin went from being valued at less than $0.25 to over $15,000 per Bitcoin.

It's easy to get excited about the hype. However, you can also easily miss out on the tremendous financial technology opportunities made possible by this technology.

In this chapter, I'm going to walk you through the promise of the Bitcoin offers by traditional financial institutions like banks, remittance companies, and transnational financial services. There's a lot to get excited about, but there's also a lot of question marks.

Don't, for a moment, think that blockchain is some sort of unqualified blessing to all parties involved. It isn't.

While the technology continues to evolve and more and more solutions are presented, there still isn't a general protocol or consensus regarding how this technology can be stabilized so that it can be applied across the board. This is a very important transition point that you need to be aware of.

Now, none of this information that I'm going to share with you is intended to discourage or depress you about blockchain. If you have read the other chapter of this book, it should be abundantly clear that I am optimistic about this technology.

There are just a few hurdles that need to be addressed for this technology to truly deliver a tremendous amount of value to people in both the developed and developing worlds.

Blockchain financial technology applications in a nutshell

Why would banks want to invest in a blockchain infrastructure for their digital ledgers? As you already know, banks operate using electronic records.

The cash that you take out of the ATM is dictated and determined by electronic records. These electronic records, in turn, are set by the Federal Reserve or centralized banking authority of the company you reside in.

I'm not going to go into the fine details of how "money is created". However, please understand the basic point that these credits exist through government fiat.

The old idea that the Federal Reserve in the United States and the Central Bank Authority in places like Europe, and other individual cities throughout the United States print out their money in antiquated way.

In the United States, most of the money that is authorized to exist is purely in digital form. The green pieces of paper that you see printed are just a fraction of the total money that actually exists.

I just want to throw that out there so you have a good background of what banks are dealing with. Now, the issue is how you go from that system to a blockchain-based system. What are the benefits of blockchain technology bring to the table when it comes to financial services?

Moving money suffers less friction

One of the biggest hassles with moving money from one jurisdiction to another involve bank-to-bank transactions. There are different fees, changing fees, changing foreign exchange rates, and a lot of other transaction related costs.

If you've ever wired money from the United States to another country or withdrew money from PayPal deposited by a customer who paid in a different currency, you would know what I'm talking about. For the cash to get you, it has to go through many different hurdles.

At each level, there are fees to be paid. There are costs taken out. By the time the money gets to you, it's not the "full amount". This happens all the time in the world of global remittances.

As more and more immigrants go the United States, Canada, Western Europe, a large percentage of them send money back home. There's a tremendous market for remittances.

Unfortunately, this is a market that is often marked by high transaction costs. This is a golden opportunity for financial technology companies to reduce these additional costs.

By making remittances as friction-free as possible, blockchain technology can make remittances dirt cheap. How much cheaper?

Well, you can send hundreds of thousands of dollars and pay less $20 to $50 in transaction costs. That's how efficient peer-to-peer blockchain-based transnational remittance system can be. In fact, people are already sending Bitcoin and paying very little in transaction fees.

Now, here's a problem. Sending cryptocurrency in of itself is not the issue. You can send Bitcoin from wallet A to wallet B with absolutely no hitch. There's absolutely no drama involved.

There's no reason to charge a high transfer fee. So far so good, right? Here's the problem. At some point down the road, you're going to have to transform or convert that Bitcoin into U.S. dollars, Canadian dollars, Japanese yen, euro, or whatever local currency you normally deal with.

You're going to have to use an online exchange for that. The exchange would then give you the going rate for the cryptocurrency that you're using.

It doesn't really matter whether you're using Bitcoin, Ethereum, Ripple, or any other popular cryptocurrency. Your funds have to go through a conversion process. This is where things get a little bit dicey.

If you've been playing or speculating on Bitcoin, you probably already know that its price goes up and down. It goes though really wild price swings.

As of this writing, Bitcoin's price can total to several hundred dollars. It's anybody's guess how much your funds would be worth once the transaction is verified at the receiver's end.

You're presented with two options. If it turns out that Bitcoin took a dive after you sent your Bitcoin, the recipient would have to wait for the value to recover. That's the negative scenario.

There's also a happy scenario when you agree to how much Bitcoin you're going to pay. After you pay the Bitcoin, it may turn out that Bitcoin is trading at a much higher rate.

This is a happy situation because your buyer may have only contracted for $1000 worth of Bitcoin, but by the time you can redeem the Bitcoin at a coin exchange, the Bitcoin may be worth $1200 or more.

Do you see how this works? This sounds awesome if you are on the receiving end of a nice price appreciation, but this causes a lot of headaches because both parties have to wait.

The recipient is essentially taking a risk-taking Bitcoin. As awesome as Bitcoin is and as solid as its cryptocurrency brand may be, it does come with baggage. It does come with a tremendous amount of uncertainty.

Traditional banks' electronic transaction solution

It's obvious that a freely traded cryptocurrency is going to be problematic when it comes to foreign exchange transactions. I don't see banks rushing to buy up a tremendous amount of Bitcoin so they can simplify their foreign exchange operation.

That's just not going to happen anytime soon. Instead, what's more likely is a scenario where huge banks like Citibank or HSBC, with a tremendous network of foreign and domestic branches, would use blockchain technology to reduce their in-house costs.

Basically, instead of sending their electronic financial data and settling it the way they currently do, blockchain may be able to provide a distributed, secure, decentralized, and relatively friction-free infrastructure. This can enable huge banks to reduce their internal costs.

Keep in mind that these costs are purely internal. We're talking about moving information from branch to branch, from one end of a country to another or from one country to another country. However, if the recipient has another bank, then there will be additional costs.

That is unavoidable, unless of course, these big banks form some sort of consortium or some giant interoperating network that leverages their reduced internal processing costs and agree to limit their costs. That can happen too.

However, the more immediate scenario would probably turn to large banks setting up a blockchain network that covers their whole global operation. It doesn't matter whether they have branches in Los Angeles, San Francisco, Mexico, the Philippines, Singapore, or Japan.

Everything is routed through this distributed network. The great thing about using blockchain for this is the fact that the system is secure.

It's constantly validating itself. It's constantly running internal checks with each transaction to ensure the integrity of the shared general ledger.

Also, the fact that this network is otherwise closed to the general public adds a much welcome layer of security. OF course, the big drawback to this involves extra hardware.

You have to understand that unlike Bitcoin, these nodes running this blockchain software must be under the full control and ownership of the bank that runs the network. The great thing about Bitcoin is that its network is so huge.

The people running the Bitcoin open source blockchain software has something to gain. They can mine Bitcoin or they can make money off the Bitcoin transaction costs shared throughout the network.

There's something in it for them. In the private blockchain scenario, all the nodes are run by one company. The whole distributed network exists for the benefit of one corporate entity.

This means that one of the greatest advantages of Bitcoin's blockchain implementation which is a shared and distributed hardware cost infrastructure isn't available. Corporate financial companies who implement this technology only stand to benefit in terms of security and redundancy.

However, they don't benefit in terms of distributed costs because they're going to be shouldering all the cost. That is a big disadvantage.

The good news is the heavy competition in the global website hosting industry has made building a distributed network using a wide range of data centers located all over the planet so much more affordable. In fact, the price of hosting a website and managing data continues to drop year after year.

That's how much competition there is. This is a good offset. If financial services company like a bank or an international remittance company were to adopt a distributed blockchain-based processing infrastructure, it can do so for a relatively affordable price.

This is not cost prohibited. So, it's possible for a big bank like Citibank to put up thousands of nodes located all over the world. Given the way the data center pricing is going, they stand to either spend the same amount of money that they're already spending for their intranet.

Key drawbacks

This internalized private blockchain infrastructure network for financial service companies is indeed exciting. However, there are two key roadblocks they need to overcome.

First is interoperability. In other words, banks have to be able to talk to each other electronically when it comes to financial transactions. This has to happen regardless of whether they use blockchain-based technology or another kind of technology.

The good news here is as more and more banks switch to an internal-based blockchain infrastructure, it would not be all that hard to line these networks together. In fact, this already exists.

If you were to go to Tokyo, Japan and try to take out money using your ATM card from New York, you'll be able to do so because there are global networks that specialize in international financial transactions. The legal and logistical work for a purely interoperable and integrated multibank blockchain infrastructure is already set in place.

The lawyers who got that network together through legal agreements only need to do a search and replace for certain provisions in the contract that enable bank ATM networks to talk and transact with each other. If they can do that with ATM, they can do that with blockchain transaction backbone system.

This should not be a problem. In fact, if banks do determine that blockchain can enable them to save a lot of money in internal costs, this can lead to smoother and faster intrabank and interbank transactions.

So instead of having to jump though many different hoops for financial transactions using the blockchain and its transparent ledger that's hard to hack and alter, banks can be more competitive. Please keep in mind that this is very different from the Bitcoin scenario.

In this scenario, we're not dealing with any kind of cryptocurrency. There's nothing to be converted except for the actual fiat cash in the network.

This means that just as your withdrawal of yen from an ATM in Tokyo, Japan would have to factor in today's U.S. dollar to yen exchange rate, you're going to have to use that same exchange rate despite the fact that the network is now powered by blockchain.

In other words, from purely surface appearances, it's as if nothing has changed. The only difference is the underlying technology that moves all those digital data back and forth, switched from the technology banks are using to highly encrypted, highly distributed, and decentralized blockchain technology.

The problem of regulation

Whenever the government gets involved, things can go crazy. Believe me, large corporations are studying Bitcoin very closely, but they haven't quite made the leap yet.

There's a lot to get excited about, but the problem is regulation. You have to understand that when governments get involved, they usually justify their regulation based on some consumer protection rationale.

It's all about protecting the consumers. It's all about protecting the integrity of the whole financial system, on and on it goes.

With block chain, the big issue that keeps coming up, as far as the noises being made by regulators in Korea, Southeast Asia, the

European Union, and North America, all boils down to security. Just how secure is a blockchain-based system?

Now, we're talking about blockchain implementations that are in-house. In other words, we're dealing with dollars to dollars and we're not dealing with any cryptocurrency. It's just fiat currency to fiat currency. It comes in dollars, it comes out yen. It comes in euro, and it comes out dollars.

Even in this environment, regulators would want to be reassured that it's going to be very secure. The more they insist, the more standards they push, or the more protocols they impose, then the costlier any Bitcoin implementation would be.

Often times, when the government gets involved, there are all sorts of documentary requests. This is actually part of what jacks up the cost of doing business.

If you are going to be placed in a position where you have to fill out a form at the end of every month or track certain pieces of data with every transaction, all these bits and pieces of activity can and do add up.

Individually, it seems like you're just doing an extra step. Given how big your network is and the tremendous size of the transactions, it would seem that this is really not that big of a deal.

However, when you scale this up to cover your whole operations and your interactions with other large players, this can translate to a lot of time, and yes, money. Make no mistake. The more labor you devote to a particular activity, the more likely your costs will go up.

They do tend to go hand-in-hand. It's still an open question how blockchain systems will be regulated. It's a big enough headache dealing with a regional regulator like the United States or the European Union, but things get a little more complicated and costlier when another regulators step in.

This is not necessarily a deal-killer. However, it can put internal roadblocks that may be so pronounced or so repetitive that it might push banks to do cost benefit analysis.

It would not be surprising for a lot of large banks, looking to squeeze every red cent worth of extra profit from their operations through streamlining, to stop or take a step back. Seriously, they understand the upside of blockchain technology.

The problem is when the factor in the regulatory costs and the additional expense of paperwork, they might hesitate. Their return on investment for removing as much of the friction out of their current system may not be high enough to make the transition worth the hassle and the cost.

This is one of those situations where too much regulation can actually hinder technological evolution. There has to be some sort of tipping point where it makes sense for large-scale financial services companies to make the transition.

The cost of being left behind is simply too high for them to tolerate. They must be made to feel that they're leaving so much money on the table that there's really no other choice, but to step up and make the transition to a fully blockchain-based internal transaction system.

The Big Promise

So, what is the big promise of a blockchain-based global financial network? Let me look into my crystal ball here.

Assuming that the regulation issue is taken care of and all the internal cost issues are addressed, what is the big benefit here? Well, first of all, by using a distributed network, big banks no longer have to worry about their records being destroyed by one single catastrophic event.

Since they will have records all over the planet, thanks to blockchain technology, they can be rest assured that regardless of what happens at one particular part of the world, it is business as usual for them. Just like the internet, when a particular part of the network comes down, everything else is rerouted.

The same applies to a blockchain-based distributed processing network. Even if 50% of the network goes down, the other 50% carries on. This is very reassuring. This is exactly the kind of peace of mind bank operators are looking for.

Also, the system verifies itself. This is not just a routing system, mind you. If that's the case and all that needs to be done is to move data from point A to point B, then banks really don't have a reason to switch to blockchain.

They can do that perfectly fine with today's technology. There's no need to transition to a blockchain system.

Instead, the internal verification system made possible by many different computers, operating together as a network and providing a centralized proof for transactions that all other computers plugged into the network would recognize, saves a lot of money. Given the fact, this cannot be taken down because it provides a self-sustaining infrastructure that is extremely scalable.

The Bottom Line

The benefits blockchain technology brings to financial transaction companies and global banks cannot be underestimated. These benefits are truly colossal. They're a big deal.

However, the challenges mentioned above have to be overcome for these institutions to logically and rationally make the switch. This is going to be quite a transition.

Not surprisingly, the numbers have to be there. This has to make sense not just today, but long into the future. The good news is blockchain technology has so much going for and it's still undergoing a tremendous amount of fine-tuning and optimization.

I'm confident that more and more financial service companies will adopt blockchain as their backbone data processing technology. Please keep in mind that all these have nothing to do with the current, as well as future health of Bitcoin.

A lot of people are under the mistaken impression that Bitcoin represents or embodies everything about blockchain. Nothing can be further from the truth.

Bitcoin is one implementation of blockchain technology. In fact, it has been criticized as an out-of-date, overly slow, and inherently problematic implementation of blockchain.

Maybe that's going too far. Maybe that's overstating the weakness of Bitcoin. The jury is still out on that, but there is one thing that we can all agree on.

We can all agree that Bitcoin is an implementation of blockchain. Blockchain itself has many different points of innovation. The more open it is, the stronger the underlying technology will be.

It doesn't really matter whether you're going to be using a blockchain infrastructure and backbone technology to distribute files all over the internet and put them together at some point, or you're moving a store of value to many different parts of the world. None of that really matters.

What matters is the integrity of the underlying technology. Thankfully, this is independent of what happens to Bitcoin. It may well be the case that Bitcoin crashes to the ground tomorrow, but that's not going to put the blockchain genie back in the bottle.

As the old saying goes, "Once the toothpaste is out of the tube, it's out there for better or worse." For better or worse, blockchain technology is out there.

Given the huge open market for innovation distributed in many parts of the world, there's a frenetic amount of activity centered on improving blockchain and adapting it to a wide range of purposes.

Make no mistake. It's a digital ledger. That much is true, but there's so many ways you can work with a digital database that it would blow your mind.

I already covered this in the previous chapter. Given how robust current developments are in speeding up blockchain transactions, tightening self-verification, and other crucial tasks, the future for this technology is definitely bright.

Conclusion

While the jury is still out on whether Bitcoin will continue to remain a store of value for currency purposes, one thing is clear: blockchain technology works! If you are looking for an example of how blockchain technology revolutionizes ledger technology, just look at Bitcoin. If for no other reason, Bitcoin has already proven itself as a 'proof of concept' regarding what blockchain can do.

Government actions might end up pushing Bitcoin to an early death. Bitcoin's value might be overtaken by other leaner and faster blockchain-based cryptocurrency 'flavors.' It can suffer a hundred different fates. Still, the genie is out of the bottle and enterprising business people such as yourself, you still have a lot of room to work with as far as blockchain innovations go.

We're only beginning to scrape at the tip of the massive iceberg of potential blockchain applications. It would be quite interesting to see the explosion of distributed computing platforms using the technology behind Bitcoin.

By reading this book, you will have the information you need to get on the blockchain wagon and help conceptualize apps that use this technology. In effect, you can help steer it to its ultimate destination.

Best Regards,
David Morales

Preview of

Stock Market

Investing

For Beginners

Simple Stock Investing Guide To Become An Intelligent
Investor And Make Money In Stocks

By David Morales

Available on Amazon

http://geni.us/stockmarket

Introduction

This is my personal stock trading story: I started trading stocks when I got my first part time job while I was still in college. You might think that this was a pretty great start. After all, most people never really start stock investing until they are already established in their careers. In fact, the average American trades stock primarily as a passive investor as part of that person's 401k plan at work. Put simply, most people don't actively look to invest in stocks.

You might think that I had a great early start with investing. Well, not quite. While Microsoft, Apple, Cisco and other amazing companies were trading at the time I started investing in stocks, I didn't invest in those stocks. If I did, I'd be worth hundreds of millions of dollars today. In fact, when I started investing, Cisco, Apple and Microsoft were trading at very low prices.

What I did was I just dove into stock investing and bought whatever "cheap" companies were being recommended by investment "experts" featured in the newspapers I read at that time. I only paid attention to two factors: the price of the stock and where it was in its 52 week valuation. If the stock was trading near its 52 week low, and the stock was affordable as far as my budget was concerned, I bought the stock.

I did not look into its industry, I did not do research regarding the company's market position. In many cases, I didn't even know if the company was making any money. I only looked at whether it was recommended by experts and whether it was cheap enough. Every pay check I would set aside a few hundred dollars to buy these "cheap" stocks I was told had a "tremendous upside."

As I mentioned, I didn't bother to do thorough industry research, nor did I pay attention to the stock's momentum, volume and other crucial trading details. The result? Of the 5 companies I invested in, 2 went bankrupt. One is still around, but it's a dormant "shell" company that is a penny stock. To make matters worse, it barely trades. The other two companies that I bought, I ended up selling them for prices that were lower than I bought them for.

Fast Forward to Today

Now, I make money on all my trades. I know when to buy in, and I know when to sell. In fact, it has become quite predictable to me. While I don't always rack up daily profits in the 5 digit range, I definitely have come a very long way from when I began trading. I actually make a profit every single day.

I've got some great news for you: if I can go from a hype-crazed foolish investor throwing good money after bad on lousy stocks to someone who can reliably pick winning stocks, so can you. The only difference between you and me is information.

This book spells out the information you need to begin your stock trading career the right way. Don't begin it the same way I did. I lost money. I worked hard for that money while I was going to college and all that money just went up in smoke. Learn from my mistakes.

Indeed, this book is a compilation of the hard lessons I've learned trading stocks through the years. Put simply, I focused on the things that work. I focused on the information you need to pay attention to so you can become a successful stock trader.

There are Tons of Investment Books Out There

Let's just get one thing out of the way, while it's true that this book is yet another of many stock investment books in the marketplace, most of those stock investment books have it all wrong. This book is intended to help newbie traders such as you to cut through the hype and fluff and get to the good stuff as quickly as possible.

You need to avoid my mistakes and benefit from what I got right. By getting the right information from the very beginning, you put yourself in a better position. You increase your chances of trading profitably, consistently. I can't emphasize the word "consistently" enough.

Make no mistake about it, anybody can get lucky from time to time. Unfortunately, luck is not going to put food on the table. Luck can fall short. You need a clear idea as to what works so you can trade with a higher chance of consistent profit.

Stock Trading is a Journey

I wish I could tell you that, just by reading this book, you will become a millionaire. Unfortunately, nobody can make that guarantee. You have to understand that stock trading is a journey. Just like any trip, it involves growth. It involves changing your perspective and, yes, it involves overcoming challenges.

This book steps you through the jungle of confusing "stock market talk" and terms and puzzling "strategies." Instead, I explain strategies in clear, everyday English, so you can make truly informed decisions when looking for trading opportunities, timing your buying and selling, and reinvesting your profits.

I wish you the very best in your journey into the amazing and richly rewarding world of stock trading!

Chapter 1: Stop! Read This Before You Start

Before you get all excited about diving into this book and putting it into action, I need to stop you in your tracks. You can't just jump in with both feet and start opening online brokerage accounts and trading away. It doesn't work that way. You have to make sure that you have the preliminary steps out of the way. Otherwise, you're simply doing things randomly and you're doing things based on emotion.

While I appreciate the fact that you are excited about this whole venture, it's too easy to trade impulsively. It's too easy to make investment decisions that aren't based on facts. It's crucial that you make sure that you have the basics out of the way so you can increase your chances of being successful in stock trading.

Please pay attention to the following questions. They will help you get prepared properly for your journey into stock trading.

Do You Have the Time to Research?

Make no mistake about it, when it comes to stock trading, you have to research and you have to do it right. This takes time. Most people think they know how to research, but it turns out that they have no clue. You have to give yourself the time and the space to do adequate research on the stocks that you will be buying or research on stock trading strategies.

There are certain strategies that don't require you to research the stock. You only need to pay attention to the volume and trader activity in that stock. The key question here is whether you have the time to do proper research on whatever trading strategy you're going to be pursuing so you can increase your chances of being successful.

Are You Curious Enough?

A lot of people read books because they're desperate for information. They just look at books to solve a problem. Now, there's nothing wrong with that, but if you really want to take things to a much higher level as far as your trading success goes, you have to be curious.

You can't just look for information, you also have to pay attention to the implications. You also have to be curious as to how to connect the dots and whether knowing one piece of information can lead to another piece of information. That's how you can learn powerful strategies in no time at all. It all depends on your curiosity.

For people who aren't curious, all of this can be a chore. It can be a hassle for them. Their hearts are not in it and they're only doing it because they need to make money quickly. I hope you can see the difference. If you're curious, you are more likely to come up with interesting solutions as well as spot potential problems. This leads to you being able to identify greater opportunities.

Do You Have Funds Ready to Invest?

This part is really important. If you want to trade in stock, you need to make sure that you have proper capital. Do you have money to invest now? If not, when will you be ready?

Don't Expect to Hit a Homerun the First Time You Step Up to the Plate and Swing the Bat!

This should be quite obvious. I'm sure the first time you played basketball, you didn't expect that you're going to play like Michael Jordan on the court. Most people don't have that expectation.

However, you'd be surprised as to how many people think that just because they're trading in stocks that their investments are going to be all winners. It doesn't work that way. In many cases, your expectations can end up sabotaging you. So, do yourself a big favor and make sure that your expectations are realistic.

What is the most realistic expectation you should have? Expect to learn. That is always my mindset and it has never let me down. You need to set the right expectations, otherwise, you might become so discouraged by your results that you end up quitting. I'm sure you already know that the only way you can fail is to quit. That's the only way you can lose.

Be Clear About Your Initial Goals

It's really important at this stage to also be clear as to why you're investing. This is really important. What are your goals? What are you going to do with the money that you will make?

This, of course, turns on how old you are. If you are somebody who is 50 years old and is a decade or slightly more away from retirement, your investment goals are going to be vastly different than if you were 22 years old and fresh out of college, or a 19-year-old and you just graduated high school.

Age matters when setting up investment goals because you can afford to take a lot more risks when you are younger. How come? Well, if you were like me and you invested in really speculative stocks when you were 19, even if all your stocks tanked, you still have a lot of time for you to get the capital together and try again.

This is not the case if you are 50 years old and you're looking at 15 more years until you retire. In that particular situation, it pays to be a little bit more conservative. Do you see the difference? It can take quite a while for you to raise the money again from your work or other sources of income.

Keep this is mind, your age has a big impact on what your investment goals and investment styles should be.

Investing for Retirement Vs. Investing for Growth

If you're investing for retirement, you're basically just looking for a reliable growth rate. This is not super sexy, you're not going to be greeted by eye popping returns that blow away the market average. Instead, you just want a steady return that beats inflation. Put simply, you have money now that you have saved through all those years of working and you want to make sure that your money retains its value long after you've retired. This is why investing for retirement is focused primarily on conservative investments like utility stocks and blue-chip stocks.

On the other hand, if you are younger, you can invest for growth. This investment goal involves investing in companies that are very speculative or maybe unpredictable. Your main focus is to grow your money as quickly as possible while, of course, accepting the risks that go with such amazing growth.

These two scenarios spell out the different investment goals people have. But if this is your first time investing, your initial goal should be to simply learn. That's right. When you open that brokerage account and you start trading, tell yourself that the way you're going to measure profits or loss is based on how much you learned. This way, you don't get terribly disappointed if your trades don't pan out. Again, it's all about expectations.

Why do you Need to Invest?

Let me cut straight to the chase. Regardless of whether you're a conservative investor that is soon going to go into retirement or you're a young person just out of high school or college, you need to know why you need to invest. This is really important because a lot of people think that stock investing is just another option out there besides saving.

Well, they are two totally different things. A lot of people are under the mistaken assumption that as long as they save money from their income and set aside a certain percentage religiously, month after month, year after year, decade after decade, they will be fine. I'm sorry to disappoint you, but that is not a winning strategy.

In fact, you are playing the game to lose if you are just going to rely on your savings. Why? There is this thing called inflation. Put in the simplest terms possible, inflation is an economic effect where the amount of goods and services one dollar buys this year is going to be worth less next year and the year after that, and so on and so forth. Ultimately, you reach a point where your dollar is no longer able to buy much of anything.

If you think this is crazy or far-fetched, you only need to realize that back in the 1800's, a full-time salary for somebody was a few dollars per month. Obviously, people can't live on that now. That just goes to show you the power of inflation because a dollar back in 1860 is worth so much more now in terms of today's dollar's purchasing power. That's how bad inflation can be.

Even if you looked at as recently as 10 years ago, the food that you could have bought back then, you can no longer buy now. For example, if you walk into a Taco Bell and spend money on a burrito, that money that you spent 10 years ago, is probably not going to buy the same amount of burritos today.

Inflation is a serious problem and simply saving money is not going to fix it. You have to find a way to grow your money. This is why stocks are so hot. Stock investing enables you to beat inflation.

If inflation is going up at a rate of 2-5% a year, you can rest on the fact that, if you put your money in a general stock fund that tracks the market index, your money may grow 10-15% per year. In other words, you beat inflation by as much as 13% or as little as 5%. Whatever the case may be, you're still beating inflation. Your money is not losing its value.

Historically speaking, stocks have appreciated in the range of between 12% to over 15% per year. That is amazing inflation protection. While real estate can give you better returns on average, real estate also can suffer a reversal.

If you don't believe me, look at the average real estate values in the United States as a whole after the great financial crash of 2008. You'd be surprised as to how quickly million-dollar homes went down in value. While real estate, generally speaking, offers a great amount of inflation protection, you would be better off with stock investing.

Advantages of Stocks over Real Estate

Without going into too much detail, it's a much better idea to invest in stocks than real estate. While both do provide you with a large measure of inflation protection, stocks are more fluid. You can simply go online to your online brokerage and place an order to sell your stock position and you're done with it. You've cashed out of your position.

This is not the case with real estate. You have to hire a broker or agent and wait possibly months or even years to unload your property. Real estate is simply not that liquid. Also, real estate's appreciation depends primarily on location.

With stocks, you can buy a whole basket of stocks through a mutual fund and if the mutual fund management company is any good, you can at least track the performance of the general market. This is not the case with real estate. You might end up in a local real estate market that under-performs the national average quite a bit.

81

Also, in terms of the money that you need to put together to invest, it takes quite a bit of money to invest in real estate. You have to at least put up the down payment required by the bank to give you a loan for the rest of the asking price of the property that you're buying.

With stocks, you have a lot more leeway. You know, coming in, how much you will be paying. Maybe you have a tight budget, so you might want to look for stocks that are trading at fairly low prices but have a high momentum or a high growth potential.

You have a lot more freedom as far as investing in stocks is concerned. If you don't have the time to research, you can take a fairly small amount of cash and invest it in a mutual fund.

In the next chapter, I'm going to cover the concept of risk. Stay tuned because this is extremely important in helping you plan out your stock investment strategy.

Available on Amazon
http://geni.us/stockmarket

-----------------------------------End of Preview----------------------------

Preview of

Investing

For Beginners

Simple Investing Guide to Become an Intelligent Investor and Grow Your Wealth Continuously

By David Morales

Available on Amazon

http://geni.us/invest

Introduction

If you're reading this book, you have some cash saved in the bank and you're thinking of growing your money. If this is the case, then you're definitely on the right track.

You are definitely on the right track because most people don't get to that stage. In fact, according to a recent survey, most Americans are living paycheck to paycheck. In fact, if they were forced to write a check for $2,000, half of America's households cannot cut that check. That's how bad things are when it comes to savings.

So if you have some cash saved in the bank and you are looking for ways to grow that pile of money, you are definitely on the right track. You are a responsible person, you are a forward thinker, and you have the raw ingredients to make that money work for you instead of you constantly having to work for your money.

The Bad News

Now for the bad news. Regardless of how much cash you may have saved, you need to grow your money because it is losing value every single day it sits in the bank. I know this is hard to believe because the $5,000 you have in your account still says $5,000 after several months sitting in the bank. When you check your statement, it says pretty much the same amount of money.

In fact, thanks to the interest being paid to you by the bank, it seems that your money is even growing by a small fraction. Well, don't get too excited. Every year, your money is able to buy less and less goods and services. This is called inflation.

Whatever your saved dollars can buy this year, will buy less next year. And it gets worse after that. In fact, the amount of products and services your money can buy on a year to year basis continues to go down. Unless you do something, your money won't be able to buy much of anything at a particular point in the future.

If you find this all hard to believe, keep in mind that in the 1930's, you could buy a house for $1,000. You could buy a car for a couple of hundred dollars. In fact, meals can be had for pennies. That's how much the US dollar has sunk in value over the decades.

Inflation is very much real and if you are not careful, the money that you worked so hard for to save up in the bank won't be able to do you much good, thanks to inflation. The worst part to all of this is that your money might deteriorate in value to such an extent that you would be putting yourself in a really tight spot at the point in your life where you are most vulnerable. I am of course talking about your retirement.

Do yourself a big favor and prepare for a better retirement future by deciding to simply get the most value out of the hard earned dollars you have stored away.

This book explores, in broad terms, the different ways you can grow the value of the money that you have saved up. This is money that you worked hard for. This is money that you sacrificed and sweated for. Make sure that it retains its value.

In fact, you should make sure that it grows in value over time instead of being eaten up by inflation. This book will not only open your mind to the prospect of increasing the value of your money, but hopefully get you excited about the whole investment process.

Chapter 1: Understand Why You Need to Grow Your Money

In the introduction, I gave you a quick summary of why you need to grow your money. In this chapter, we're going to dive in a little bit deeper into inflation and reduction in purchasing power.

The reason why I need to drive this point home is that it's very easy to treat inflation as some sort of intellectual construct. It's easy to think of it as some sort of idea that affects other people, but passes you by. Believe me, inflation hits everybody.

In fact, inflation is so efficient that it works almost like clockwork. Unless you invested the right way, inflation will hit you. Even if you make good money now at your job, inflation will make sure that your hard earned dollars won't stretch as much as they used to. Inflation is that bad.

Saving is Great and is Crucial, But It isn't Enough

You probably are thinking that you've won most of the battle when it comes to personal financial management the moment you've learned to save. I can't say I blame you for thinking along these lines because most people can't even get around to saving. They're always looking at their expenses. They're always looking at their long term liabilities and they never really get around to saving much of anything.

If anything, savings happens at the end of the budget process. They would get their income, and then they would immediately take out

86

their expenses and their liabilities and whatever is left over maybe goes to savings, assuming it survives luxury expenses or entertainment expenses. It is no surprise that given this situation, most Americans don't even have $2,000 in the bank.

As I've mentioned in the introduction, if they were forced by circumstances to cut a check for $2,000, almost half of American households cannot cut that check. They know it's going to bounce. They know they're going to get into trouble if they issue that check. That's how bad things are on a household to household basis, as far as American personal financial management goes.

Since you are able to save, you have overcome that. You have developed a very powerful discipline that enables you to pay yourself first. A lot of people budget their income in a way where savings comes last. You and other savers, on the other hand, think differently. You pay yourself first.

What you do is you take your income and you set aside savings first and everything else that's left will be divvied up among expenses and liabilities. This is absolutely the correct way to do things. It's rough at first, it takes some getting used to, but the more you do it, the better you get at it. And I definitely congratulate you for having developed the discipline and personal financial skill to be able to pull this off.

However, as awesome as this accomplishment may be, it isn't enough. Saving is crucial for effective personal financial management, but simply saving or putting money in the bank is a losing game. Why? The 800 pound gorilla called inflation.

The Very Real Threat of Inflation

Before we get an understanding of why inflation is so bad, it's a good idea to talk about where inflation comes from. Why is it that the price of goods and services tend to rise over time?

Let's put it this way, if you walked into a Taco Bell 12 years ago, I can guarantee you that the prices on the menu look way different than their current price list. This is guaranteed. Why? Food prices, just like with everything else, tend to go up over time.

Sure, there are certain categorical exemptions, but for the most part, this is true. In fact, this applies to almost all product categories. Whether we're looking at clothing, computer items, stereo equipment, and so on and so forth, the prices of goods tend to go up over time.

However, thanks to the outsourcing of manufacturing to China, a lot of the inflationary pressure on consumer goods have dropped fairly recently. It's anybody's guess how long this will continue. We seem to have gotten quite a bit of a break, thanks to the miracles of modern globalized mass manufacturing, which enables Walmart to sell products cheaper and cheaper by the year. That is the exception that proves the rule.

For everything else, especially services, prices tend to go up over time. The reason for this is due to money supply. You have to understand that unlike the olden days, the value of money is no longer tied to a physical object.

For the longest time, the value of the US dollar, as well as other currencies, was tied to gold or, to a lesser degree, silver. There was some sort of physical frame of reference for the value of money. While governments did play fast and loose with how they arrived at the value of their money or how they fixed the value of their money, for the most part, they still had a frame of reference that is tied to a precious metal.

Since there is that link to real world industrial value as represented by that precious metal, governments can't go crazy with valuation. They can't just print out money with abandon and expect the market to take care of it. It doesn't work that way. They are forced to establish some sort of discipline because their money is at least superficially backed up by gold or some sort of precious metal.

Well, nowadays, money only has value because the issuing government behind that money says that it has value. In other words, the global economy works on a "trust me" basis. This is why when global financial traders lose confidence in a government, that government's currency crashes. Look at the case of Zimbabwe for the most recent case study of this effect.

When Zimbabwe, starting in the early 2000's, started nationalizing white-farmer owned farms, it collapsed the economy. At a certain point, the Zimbabwe government was printing out notes in trillion denominations and it still wasn't enough to buy you a dozen eggs or a loaf of bread. If this sounds familiar, it is because this happens in almost all decades to many different economies.

For example, in the 1920's, this happened in Germany. People would take a wheelbarrow, fill it up with paper cash to buy a loaf of bread. This is the real problem with money that has no confidence.

And unfortunately, when governments constantly print out billions upon billions of paper notes every single year, this has the residual effect of depressing purchasing value.

This is the real reason for inflation. It's all about money supply, as well as relative confidence in the currency, and the economy behind that currency. As you can probably already tell, there is a very real threat of inflation because it's always going up.

You have to find a way to protect the value of your money. Otherwise, regardless of how much cash you have saved up today, it's not going to buy much in the future because prices have shot through the roof.

Investing Grows Your Money

Investing grows the value of the money that you've saved up in the bank. That is the long and short of investing. The reason you're investing is because you want to end up with more than what you started. You also want to end up with more than what the bank will pay you in the form of interest.

You have to understand that keeping your money in the bank to collect interest is a losing game. Why? Not only is the interest pitifully low and always below the rate of inflation, you also get taxed on the appreciation of your money. In other words, you lose twice. That's why it's really important to make sure that you only put money in the bank as a temporary strategy while you're figuring where to ultimately invest your money.

Focus on investing your money instead of keeping it in cash form. Keeping your money in cash partially is always a good idea because you don't know what the future will bring. However, it is also always a bad idea to keep all your money in the form of cash because of inflation.

Investing enables you to grow your money. That is the core of investing. With that said, there are different ways to grow your money.

Asset Classes

Asset classes are a fancy economic term for the different kinds of ways you can grow your money. You buy assets that differ from each other and these assets, categorically speaking, have different rates of appreciation. In other words, they grow your money at different rates.

It's important to note that when people talk about "investing," they almost always talk about stocks and bonds. But these two types of assets, as big and popular as they may be, are just two of many. You can try real estate, you can try passive income businesses, you can try active businesses, you can try precious metals. There are many different ways you can grow money, and this book will step you through some of the more common investment asset classes you can get into.

Available on Amazon
http://geni.us/invest
-----------------------------------End of Preview-----------------------------

To Read David Morales' More Books, Please Visit Below URL-

http://geni.us/davidbooks

To Read David Morales Blogs, Please Visit Below URL-

https://investingmoneymastery.com

CPSIA information can be obtained
at www.ICGtesting.com
Printed in the USA
BVHW04s1147111018
529889BV00010B/118/P